HAL•LEONARD

TRUMPET PLAY-ALONG

BIG BAND CLASSICS
Featuring
Tony Scodwell

CONTENTS

Cover Photo: Mary Scodwell

ISBN 978-1-4234-4131-1

HAL•LEONARD®
CORPORATION
7777 W. BLUEMOUND RD. P.O. BOX 13819 MILWAUKEE, WI 53213

Visit Hal Leonard Online at
www.halleonard.com

NOTES FROM TONY

In a Sentimental Mood

What else is there to say about Duke Ellington that hasn't been said? I feel he is our country's greatest songwriter and "Sentimental Mood" is such a strong piece for the trumpet. The melody is perfect to showcase your best tone (with a controlled vibrato) and in a comfortable range as well. Playing unison with the trumpets at B is good in live situations for a little more impact, as is the unison with the first trumpet six bars from the end. After your last solo four bars from the end, add some "blue" notes on the last chord down to low G (Gm7♭5).

King Porter Stomp

Pretty much the same chart that all the great big bands played through the years. You have lead after the four-bar drum kick off. Play this with a strict time feeling, perhaps a bit "on top" of the beat. It's part of the heritage of this music to play it with the same concept as it was originally done. It has three trumpets trading fours at C with you leading off. Walter Blanton and Rocky Lombardo are your partners here. After Jay Rasmussen plays his tenor solo at E, followed by some ensemble playing, you play lead at H and the last four bars. Your ending "F" is over the first trumpet's "E♭", which is sometimes a little hard to hear. Get it in your ear first and it'll be a breeze.

Memories of You

A trumpet feature for two down front. I used to call them part A (alto) and part H (high), but changed them to part A and B to keep it simple. I recorded both parts doing part A first. When recording part B, I was sorry to have held the last note so long on the previous take. Tank up for the G. It would be fun to play through this with a friend on the other part. Stay fairly close to what's written.

Peace

This arrangement, written by Frank Mantooth, was a perfect vehicle for Rocky Lombardo to display why he's considered such a leading jazz soloist. Believe it or not, it's quite close to what Mantooth wrote. Rocky just makes this a personal vehicle for his artistry. I threw a few cues, sat back and was amazed as usual with his playing.

Samba de Orfeu

At the time Dick Wright arranged this for me, I was going to Brazil to play with a big band there. For sure it is "in the samba mode," but it is a comfortable fit for an American trumpet-playing bandleader as well. Stay with what's written, play with good time and it flows like a good samba should.

Take the "A" Train

This arrangement by Everette Longstreth is a feature for both the trumpet-playing bandleader in the written out solo spots at B and H, plus other soloists in the band from letter C through E which can be an open solo section. In this case Fred Haller plays one chorus followed by Rocky Lombardo. You have lead over the ensemble at F and G, which is to be played as written.

Things Ain't What They Used to Be

Lots of ensemble and tenor (Jay Rasmussen) before you pick up the plunger at F. For me, the definitive solo on this old warhorse was played by Snooky Young. In my opinion, Snooky was the greatest trumpet player to ever sit in the lead chair. Just listen to the Basie and the Thad Jones/Mel Lewis recordings for starters. Young's concept of time was flawless but loose at the same time. I've taken the liberty of copying Snooky's solo pretty much verbatim. Why mess with perfection? Letter H is some flash over the band to take this chart out with energy. Have fun and pace yourself.

TONY SCODWELL BIG BAND PERSONNEL

Trumpet/Leader: Tony Scodwell

Trumpets: Tom DiLibero (lead), Rocky Lombardo, Walter Blanton, Tom Snelson

Trombones: Walter Boenig (lead), Kevin Stout, Sonny Hernandez

Saxes: Fred Haller (lead alto), Sam Pisciotta (alto), Jay Rasmussen (tenor), Tony Osiecki (tenor), Gary Freyman (bari)

Piano: Ruth Lombardo

Bass: Ken Seiffert

Drums: Clyde Duell

Tony Scodwell plays trumpets and flugelhorns of his own design, the SCODWELL USA.
Tom DiLibero, Rocky Lombardo and Walter Blanton play SCODWELL USA trumpets.

IN A SENTIMENTAL MOOD

By Duke Ellington

PEACE

Words and Music by Horace Silver

Solo B♭ Flugelhorn

KING PORTER STOMP

By Ferd "Jelly Roll" Morton

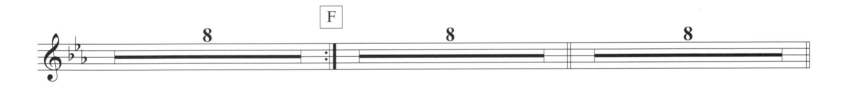

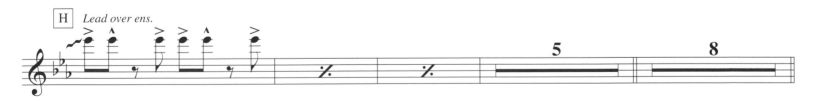

MEMORIES OF YOU

Lyric by Andy Razaf
Music by Eubie Blake

Solo B♭ Trumpet A

MEMORIES OF YOU

Lyric by Andy Razaf
Music by Eubie Blake

Solo B♭ Trumpet B

SAMBA DE ORFEU

Words by Antonio Maria
Music by Luiz Bonfa

TAKE THE "A" TRAIN

Words and Music by Billy Strayhorn

Solo B♭ Trumpet

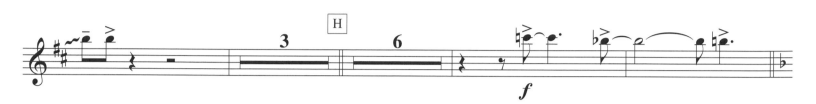

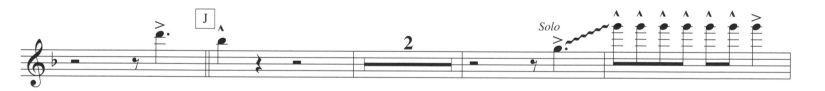

THINGS AIN'T WHAT THEY USED TO BE

By Mercer Ellington

Solo B♭ Trumpet